FUTURE PERFECT

FUTURE PERFECT

HOW TO *profit* FROM YOUR PENSION PLANNING

GYLES BRANDRETH
asks the questions

NATIONAL ASSOCIATION OF PENSION FUNDS
gives the answers

Robson Books

Design: Clive Sutherland
Design concept and cover design: Craig Dodd

First published in Great Britain in 1988 by Robson Books Ltd,
Bolsover House, 5–6 Clipstone Street, London W1P 7EB.

British Library Cataloguing in Publication Data

Future perfect: how to profit from your
pension planning.
1. Great Britain. Superannuation schemes
I. Brandreth, Gyles, *1948-* II. National
Association of Pension Funds
331.25'2'0941

ISBN 0-86051-515-X

Printed in Great Britain by Billing & Sons Ltd., Worcester

The National Association of Pension Funds Limited

Formed in 1923, the National Association of Pension Funds has become the authoritative voice of the UK pensions movement. The Association represents the pensions interests of nearly two thirds of the country's workforce in employer pension schemes and plays a leading role in encouraging provision of effective pension benefits.

Contents

Acknowledgements

Without the National Association of Pension Funds this book couldn't have been written. Among the NAPF Secretariat Colin Steward and Richard Fairclough laboured long and arduously to unravel the many intricacies of pensions law and strategy, so that they could be explained in layman's language. Ted Drake, a member of the Association's Parliamentary Committee, gave generously of his time, working through draft after draft and never failing to make perceptive and important improvements to each. At the hub of the whole daunting project stands Michael Elton, Director General of the National Association of Pension Funds, who was bold enough to undertake this awesome task in the first place, and whose wise counsel and clarity of thought in sifting through a myriad of complexities is evident on every page.

Opportunity Knocks

Has anyone told you that the financial opportunity of a lifetime is waiting to be seized – right now – by you and me and millions of men and women like us? It's one we'll be able to benefit from straightaway and right through to the ends of our days. It won't have us filling in football pools coupons, feverishly anticipating an ERNIE jackpot, or chancing our savings on anything that runs on four legs. No – what's on offer is real, rock solid and ours for the taking.

It's our pension – and now we're being given the chance to pick the perfect one and turn it into a bright golden future for ourselves and our families. What's more the choice is wholly ours and we can often tailor whichever we choose so that it suits our changing needs and circumstances.

The mention of pensions immediately brings retirement to mind – and what a retirement, if we make the right provisions. Imagine having the money as well as the free time to spend doing all those things that working life restricted. Imagine being free of financial worries and really able to enjoy what may amount to a quarter of our lives confident that whatever happens we and our families will be fully protected. Think of the places we'd be able to visit, the interests old and new we'd be able to pursue and above all the sheer fun we'd have if we really profit from our pension planning.

It's not just financial security in retirement that's on offer. Thanks to special tax advantages we can reduce the amount of tax we pay while we're at work and add to our retirement income. Then there's the life insurance and financial security a pension can provide even before we retire. So we really can begin to benefit from day one.

Why has all this come about? Important changes have been made in pensions legislation which are throwing open this exciting range of choices and opportunities. Arriving at the right decision is exhilarating if it's approached systematically. And by following a methodical progress we can weigh all the pros and cons and listen to guidance from various sources without ever losing sight of our prime objective – finding the pension that's going to ensure a perfect future!

That's just what this book helps us do.

Here the key issues and options are presented in a clear, accurate, matter of fact way by leading pension experts – the National Association of Pension Funds. But this is very much a book for you and me. It's our views, our personal cicumstances and needs that lie at its heart. We're presented with important questions about ourselves and our plans – with plenty of space to record our answers. There are probing questions too for us to put to pension advisers at work and from the pension's industry outside. And as we work our way through, gradually piecing together the perfect pensions package, there are tips and hints reminding us not to overlook details which might change in the years ahead.

In your hands you're holding a handbook for action – so get cracking and chart the course that's really going to make your future perfect!

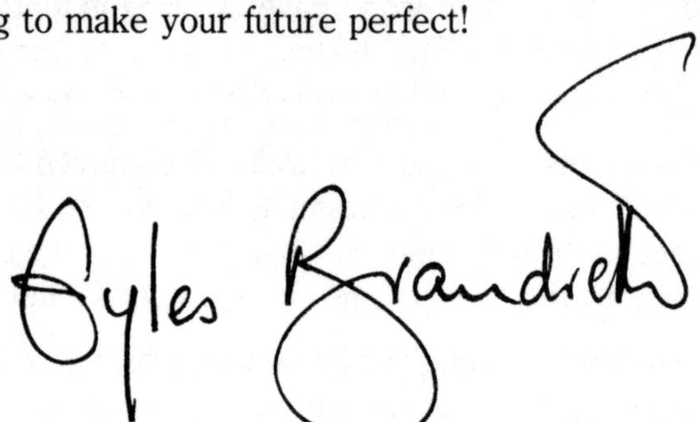

Gyles Brandreth

FUTURE PERFECT

What types of pension scheme are there?

For the sake of clarity it's worth listing what we're actually going to be looking at in the following pages.

There are three types of pension...

The State Scheme
This is in two parts:

i) The State basic pension (the 'old age pension')
ii) The State Earnings Related Pension (called SERPS)

Employer Schemes
These come in three main types...

i) Final salary schemes
ii) Money purchase schemes
iii) Hybrid schemes

Personal Pensions
There are three types of these too...

i) Deposit types
ii) With-profit types
iii) Unit-linked types

The State Scheme

The State basic pension (the 'old age pension')

As the State basic pension is generally known as the 'old age pension', we'll be calling it that from now on.

The old age pension is the same for everyone – an amount that's roughly equivalent to a fifth of average earnings in the country as a whole. For a married couple it's nearly a third of average earnings. And if both a husband and wife have worked and earned an old age pension in their own right, they each get a fifth of average earnings.

Once it starts to be paid, the old age pension keeps up with increases in the retail price index, which from now on we'll call 'the rise in prices' or 'inflation'.

The old age pension is provided from National Insurance contributions which must be paid by both employers and employees. When they retire, employees qualify for the full old age pension provided enough contributions have been paid – if they haven't the pension is reduced.

Men start to be paid their old age pension when they reach 65, women when they are 60. A widow also gets an old age pension if she was over 45 (younger if she has dependent children) when her husband died. However, a widower doesn't get an old age pension unless he's earned one in his own right.

Self-employed people can have old age pensions but because they have no employers, they must pay all the National Insurance contributions themselves.

The State Earnings Related Pension (SERPS)

Since the old age pension is – as its technical name implies – of such a basic amount, SERPS is designed to supplement it.

For anyone retiring up to the end of this century, the SERPS pension can amount to up to a **further** fifth of average earnings. However, SERPS is being cut back and the pension for anyone retiring after the year 2000 will gradually become less and less.

Under SERPS married couples **don't** get a bigger pension, though both a husband and his wife can earn a SERPS pension in their own right. As with the old age pension, the SERPS pension is linked to the rise in prices and the starting dates for payment are also the same.

Employees pay extra National Insurance contributions based on their earnings between an amount roughly the same as the old age pension and seven times that amount. Up to that higher amount, the more they earn, the more they pay. And the more they pay, the bigger their SERPS pensions.

Employers also pay extra National Insurance contributions towards SERPS pensions, but they pay them on **all** an employee's earnings above the lower amount.

Widows are able to inherit part of their husbands' SERPS pensions and in some circumstances widowers inherit part of their wives'.

Self-employed people can't have a SERPS pension.

Employer Schemes

Final Salary Schemes

In a final salary scheme the employer promises to provide each employee with a pension based on his or her level of earnings at or close to retirement.

The actual proportion will depend on the length of time the employee has worked for the employer. For instance, employees may be given 1/60th of their annual earnings at or close to retirement for each year they have been with the employer. So an employee with 30 years service would be given a pension worth 30/60ths – or one half – of those earnings.

Because the employees get the benefit of a defined proportion of their earnings at or close to retirement, a final salary scheme is sometimes called a 'defined benefit' scheme.

The employer must pay a contribution for each employee to a fund covering all employees in the scheme. In most schemes the employees also contribute to the fund. The employees' contributions – if any – are based on a percentage of their earnings.

The money in the fund is invested and the employer meets the promise made to employees by paying their pensions out of the fund.

The employer's contributions must be big enough to enable him to meet his promise.

The vast majority of employees with pensions, particularly in large and medium sized companies, are in final salary schemes.

Money Purchase Schemes

With a money purchase scheme – in contrast to a final salary scheme – the employer doesn't promise to pay a **pension** of a defined amount. Instead, he only promises to pay **contributions** of a defined amount – and normally requires employees to pay defined contributions as well.

That is why this type is sometimes called a 'defined contribution' scheme.

Unlike a final salary scheme, therefore, employees in money purchase schemes can't tell with any certainty what their eventual pensions will be in relation to their earnings when they retire.

The employer's and the employee's contribution rates are usually defined as percentages of the employee's earnings.

As in a final salary scheme, the contributions are paid into a fund covering all employees in the scheme, and the fund is invested. But – unlike a final salary scheme – the part of the fund which is derived from a particular employee's contributions together with the employer's contributions for that particular employee is not absorbed into the fund as a whole. It becomes that employee's own personal 'pot'.

The employer uses this 'pot' to provide the employee with a pension in the form of a regular annual income from the time he or she retires until his or her death. The employer often provides this **annual income** by buying what's called an **annuity** – usually from an insurance company.

So the size of each employee's pension – the amount of their annual income – will depend on the size of their 'pot' when they retire. The size of this 'pot' depends on the size of the fund as a whole and that will depend how successfully – or otherwise – that fund has been invested.

Money purchase schemes are less common than final salary schemes but are becoming more popular, especially with smaller companies: an employer is not at risk of having to pay in extra to meet a promise to pay a defined amount of pension **because he has made no such promise.**

Hybrid Schemes

A hybrid scheme is a mixture of a final salary scheme and a money purchase scheme and gives the employee the opportunity to have the best of both worlds.

There are various types. Normally, the employee's pension is calculated in two ways: firstly, as if the scheme provided **just** final salary benefits and secondly as if it provided **just** money purchase benefits, as we've outlined them above.

The results of these two methods of calculation are compared and then a pension is provided on the basis of the one most favourable to the employee.

Personal Pensions

Personal pensions are individual pension plans for people who are at work, whether they are self-employed or have an employer. But if they have an employer, the general rule is that they can't belong to their employer's scheme as well as having a personal pension.

Personal pensions are arranged by individuals for themselves. They are not provided by the State as in the case of the old age pension and SERPS or by employers as in the case of employer schemes.

Personal pensions are provided by insurance companies, unit trusts, banks, building societies and friendly societies, which we'll be referring to as 'personal pension providers'.

Although they are individual pension plans, personal pensions work rather like employer money purchase schemes. When someone with a personal pension retires, the money that has built up in his or her own personal fund is used to buy a pension – again in the form of an annuity and again usually from an insurance company.

That's why it's a money purchase scheme – the size of an individual's personal fund at retirement depends on the amount of his or her contributions and how successfully they've been invested. In other words it depends on what those contributions 'purchase'. People with personal pensions can't be sure of the size of their pension because they can't know for certain what the size of their own personal funds will be.

That will depend quite a lot on which type of personal pension they choose. If you glance back to page 13 you'll see they have a choice of three:

Deposit types
The size of their funds at retirement will be the amount they have paid in plus interest.
Personal pensions like this are provided mainly by banks and building societies.

With-profit types
At retirement their funds will consist of a basic guaranteed sum plus bonuses. Bonuses, usually added once a year, depend on a provider's investment profits. Once added, bonuses can't be lost, but future bonuses aren't guaranteed.
These types are provided mainly by life assurance companies and friendly societies.

Unit-linked types
The contributions are invested in a unit trust, a means of owning shares. These tend to go up and down with the stock market, so the size of the fund at retirement can't be guaranteed at all.

Personal pensions of this type are provided mainly by unit trusts and life assurance companies.

With all three types of personal pension, part of the contributions is liable to be used to cover the expenses of the personal pension provider and perhaps commission as well.

Additional Voluntary Contributions

Employees have the right to pay extra money – over and beyond their normal contributions – into their employers' schemes in order to improve their benefits from those schemes. Since this is extra money and employees only pay it if they want to, these payments are called 'additional voluntary contributions' – AVCs for short. And because these AVCs improve benefits from employer schemes, they are called 'in-scheme' AVCs.

In addition, or as an alternative, employees can pay extra money into AVC schemes run by personal pension providers. AVC schemes like this are separate from employer schemes and so are called 'free-standing' AVC schemes. This is important, because employees can stay in their employers' schemes and, at the same time, pay AVCs into free-standing schemes, which are similar to personal pensions.

Unlike most of the standard contributions to pension schemes, employees can pay in-scheme and free-standing AVCs irregularly. For instance, if an employee gets an unexpectedly high bonus, he or she can pay a chunk of it as an AVC. Alternatively payments could be skipped for a couple of years to cover the cost of a new roof, for example.

With or Without SERPS?

Employer Schemes

An employer scheme must be additional to SERPS, so that employees get a SERPS pension as well. That's unless the employer takes the scheme out of SERPS. If this happens it's technically known as a 'contracted-out' scheme.

Employees in 'contracted-out' schemes have to give up their right to a SERPS pension. But in return both the employees and their employers pay smaller National Insurance contributions. The difference between this lower 'contracted-out rate' and the higher 'contracted-in rate' is called the 'contracting out rebate' or, as we'll call it, the 'National Insurance rebate'.

Employers can only take their schemes out of SERPS if they are at least as good as SERPS. Broadly speaking this means that, in order to be taken out of SERPS, a final salary scheme must guarantee a pension which is at least as good as the SERPS pension employees would otherwise get. And a money purchase scheme must ensure that the contributions made to the scheme are at least as big as would otherwise be made to SERPS, i.e. at least as big as the National Insurance rebate.

Free-standing AVCs and Personal Pensions

If an employer scheme is not contracted out of SERPS by the employer, individual employees may choose to take out a free-standing AVC on their own behalf and use it to contract out of SERPS themselves.

An employee with a personal pension may use this to contract out of SERPS.

If a free-standing AVC or a personal pension is used to contract out of SERPS, it replaces SERPS for the individual concerned.

In both these cases – unlike the case of 'contracted-out' employer schemes – both the individual employee and the employer must still pay full National Insurance contributions. However, the State pays the National Insurance rebate* as a minimum contribution to the free-standing AVC or the personal pension, instead of keeping it to provide a SERPS pension.

* * *

So the broad principle is that employees must:

Either be 'contracted-in' and have a SERPS pension **as well as** another pension

Or be 'contracted-out' and have another pension **instead of** a SERPS pension, ***provided*** **the other pension is at least as good as SERPS** (pension-wise for a final salary scheme – contribution-wise for a money purchase employer scheme and personal pension).

We shall call a pension scheme that is 'contracted-in' a scheme 'with' SERPS and one which is 'contracted-out' a scheme 'without' SERPS.

As people who are self-employed can't have a SERPS pension, for them the question of 'contracting-in' or 'contracting-out' doesn't arise.

* together with a small tax allowance in the case of a personal pension.

Important Footnote

The Government wishes to encourage people to leave SERPS, in order to reduce the financial burden on the State in the years to come.

From 6 April 1988 the State – in certain circumstances – will:

i) pay a 2% incentive to an employer scheme which is 'with' SERPS, to encourage the employer to take it out of SERPS.

ii) pay a 2% incentive to a free-standing AVC or a personal pension, if an individual takes out a free-standing AVC or a personal pension which is 'without' SERPS.

This incentive is 2% of the earnings on which the extra National Insurance contributions for SERPS were based.

The incentive will be used to improve the benefits of a free-standing AVC, a personal pension, or a money purchase employer scheme. In a final salary employer scheme, it can be used either to improve benefits for employees, or to reduce the employer's costs.

But the incentive will only be paid until 6 April 1993 – a maximum period of five years – though in the case of a personal pension which is taken out 'without' SERPS before 6 April 1989, the payment of the incentive can be backdated to 6 April 1987.

Take two examples:-

1 An employer scheme is taken out of SERPS on 5 April 1990 – it will receive the incentive for 3 years (from 6 April 1990 to 6 April 1993).

2 An individual takes out a personal pension which is 'without' SERPS on 5 April 1989 – he or she will receive the incentive for 4 years (from 6 April 1989 to 6 April 1993), but will also receive an extra 4% because the incentive will be backdated for 2 years to 6 April 1987.

We look forward to the 1993 edition of this book – not because the incentive will no longer be available – but because no-one will have to read this footnote!

Before we take the next step, it may be helpful to pause for a moment to consolidate the ground we've just covered by looking at two charts. They show what happens to an employee's contributions to the State scheme and a personal pension – firstly if the personal pension is 'with' SERPS and secondly if it's 'without' SERPS.

1. Personal Pension 'with' SERPS

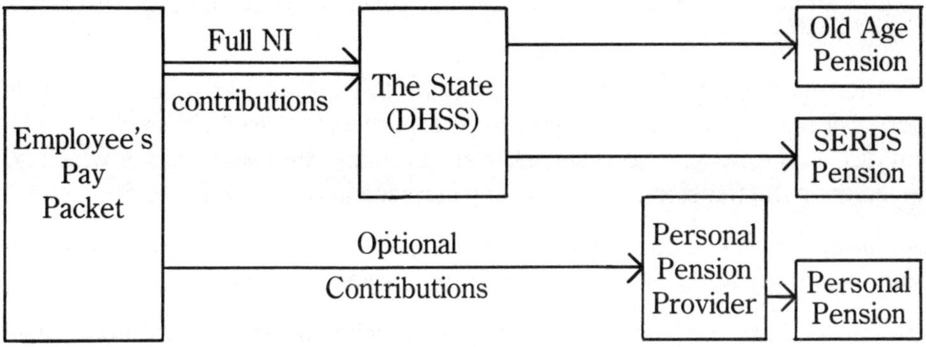

2. Personal Pension 'without' SERPS

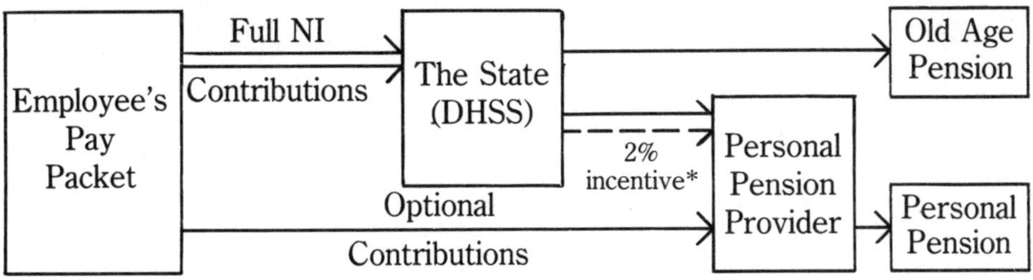

*if applicable (see Important Footnote opposite)

Footnote: You'll see that in the above charts we've shortened 'National Insurance' to 'NI' and that below 'the State' we've put in brackets 'DHSS'. This means the Department of Health and Social Security, which is the Department of State (or Government Department) that deals with these matters.

The employer also pays full National Insurance contributions which follow the same routes to the same destinations! He may or may not pay contributions to the employee's personal pension provider.

Can I Save Tax?

Yes. The effect of tax laws is that your contributions to your pension scheme – whether an employer scheme or a personal pension – are deducted from your earnings before they are assessed for income tax purposes. In other words, you get tax relief at the top rate of the income tax you pay. You don't pay tax on your employer's contributions either.

Contributing as much as possible to your pension is therefore a very good way of saving tax. But you don't get tax relief on your National Insurance contributions.

Furthermore, your employer (if you belong to an employer scheme) or your personal pension provider (if you have a personal pension) doesn't have to pay tax on the income he receives from investing the contributions which go to make up the pension fund, or on any increase in the value of the fund itself.

Naturally you pay income tax on the income from your pension in just the same way as you do on your earnings when you are working.

However, there are limits to the extent to which you can take advantage of all the big tax advantages we have described.

How Much Can I Pay In and How Much Will I Get Out?

Employer Schemes

There is a limit to the amount you can contribute to an employer scheme – 15% of your earnings.*

As explained above, you get tax relief on your contributions at the top rate of income tax you pay.**

There is a limit to the amount of pension you can have – ⅔rds of your earnings when you retire.***

You can take part of your pension as a tax-free lump sum when you retire. If you do this, your pension will of course be reduced, depending on the size of your lump sum. Usually you can take a lump sum of 3/80ths of your earnings when you retire for each year you've worked for your employer – up to a maximum of 40 years. If you multiply 3/80ths by 40, you will see that your lump sum can be 1½ times your earnings when you retire. However, there is a top limit to lump sums of £150,000.****

* This 15% limit includes anything extra you pay to an AVC scheme. It does **not** include the National Insurance rebate or the 2% incentive paid by the State to employer schemes which are 'without' SERPS. Nor does it include the 2% incentive paid by the State to a free-standing AVC which is 'without' SERPS.

** You do **not** get tax relief on the National Insurance rebate or on the 2% incentive paid by the State to a free-standing AVC which is 'without' SERPS.

*** The limit is less than ⅔rds if you have been in your employer's scheme for less than a certain length of time – normally 20 years if you joined the scheme on or after 17 March 1987, 10 years if you joined before then.

**** Unless you joined your present employer's scheme before 17 March 1987. If you've worked for your employer for less than 40 years but for at least 20 years, you may still be able to increase your lump sum to 1½ times your earnings when you retire – subject to the limit of £150,000.

Personal Pensions

Until you are over 50 the most you can pay to a personal pension is 17½% of your earnings. You're allowed to pay more when you pass 50, with the limit gradually increasing to 27½% of your earnings when you're over 60.*

Here, too, you get tax relief on your contributions at the top rate of income tax you pay.**

If your employer pays anything towards your personal pension your **combined** contributions mustn't be greater than the limits allowed for your own contributions.

There is no limit to the amount of pension you can have, except of course that you can't have more than your contributions produce.

You can take up to a quarter of the proceeds of your personal pension as a tax-free lump sum when you retire.***

The bigger the lump sum, the less you have left to pay for your pension – so that will be less.

The lump sum can't be more than £150,000.

You can actually have more than one personal pension. If you do, they must be added together for the purpose of working out the limit of your contributions. But you are allowed to take a lump sum of up to £150,000 from each of them.

* These limits do **not** include the National Insurance rebate or the 2% incentive paid by the State to a personal pension which is 'without' SERPS.

** You also get tax relief on your share of the National Insurance rebate (but not on the 2% incentive) paid by the State to a personal pension which is 'without' SERPS.

*** For this purpose the proceeds of a personal pension which is 'without' SERPS exclude the part derived from the National Insurance rebate.

Changing Jobs

Most people will change jobs several times during their working lives – sometimes to increase their earnings and job opportunities, but in some cases because they're forced to. As a result their pension entitlements may be built up in a number of different ways from different schemes.

If you're in a **final salary** scheme and leave within two years of joining it, you're entitled to have back your contributions (if any) but not those made by your employer. In this case the amount you get back is taxable, since you got tax relief on the contributions when you made them.

If you leave a final salary scheme after two years, you're entitled to the cash value of your pension rights to date. This is an amount which reflects the cost of providing the pension you've earned by that stage. For example, suppose you leave a scheme based on 1/60th for every year's service after being in it 4 years, the cash value reflects the cost of providing 4/60ths of your annual earnings at the date you leave – increased by an amount which takes some account of inflation from the time you leave the scheme to your normal retirement date.

You can transfer this cash value to your new employer scheme or to a personal pension. If you opt for your new employer's scheme, you'll often be credited with additional years of service. But in pension terms 5 years in your old scheme at your old salary may only be equivalent to 3 years in your new scheme at your new salary.

On the other hand, you can leave your pension rights to date in your old employer's scheme. If you choose to do this, your old employer won't make any further contributions, but all or part of your pension* must be given protection against inflation of 5% a year (or less if the rise in prices is less) from the time you leave until your normal retirement date.

If you're in a **money purchase** employer scheme, changing jobs is perfectly simple. You'll be able to find out exactly how much is in your personal 'pot' and when you change jobs you can simply take this to your new employer or to a personal pension.

The same applies to a **personal pension.** You'll be able to take your personal fund with you however often you change jobs. That's why personal pensions are sometimes called 'portable' pensions.

* all if you joined the scheme since 1 January 1985, otherwise at least the part of it you've earned since then.

What Choices Do I Have?

That depends on which of three situations you're in...

You're self-employed

You're employed but can't join an employer scheme

You belong to or can join an employer scheme

Now we'll have to look at each of these in turn and see what choices the law allows you to have.

SITUATION 1 – I'm Self-employed

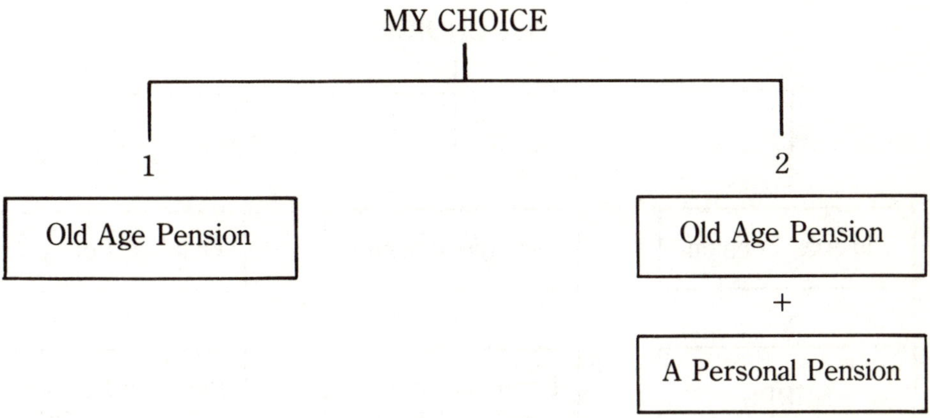

You can see at once that your choice is pretty limited.

You can't belong to an employer scheme because you haven't got an employer! We've already mentioned that you **can't** have a SERPS pension if you're self-employed so that the question of contracting your personal pension into or out of SERPS doesn't arise.

So there's only one question for you to ask.

Question: Should I choose 1 or 2?

Answer: Simple – it's better to have a personal pension as well as the old age pension, so you should choose 2.

The old age pension is most unlikely to provide the kind of income you will want in your retirement. By contributing to a personal pension, you can have the tax advantages and at the same time save up for your retirement.

We explained on page 14 that you must pay all the National Insurance contributions for your old age pension yourself as you haven't got an employer to pay any. You must also pay all the contributions to your personal pension yourself.

SITUATION 2 – I'm employed but can't join an employer scheme

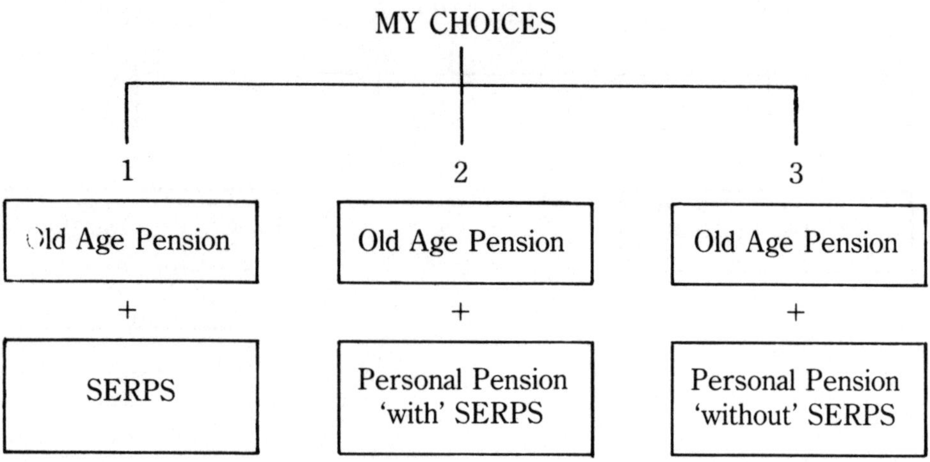

Here your decision becomes a bit more complicated. Although you have an employer, he hasn't got an employer scheme or only has one you can't join. But being employed (as opposed to self-employed), you **can** have a SERPS pension to supplement the old age pension and therefore you **can** contract your personal pension into or out of SERPS.

So in this situation there's more than one choice.

FIRST CHOICE

Let's first assume you don't want to contribute more than you have to. In that case, your choice is between 1 and 3.

You'll remember that in both cases you pay full National Insurance contributions.

In 1 the National Insurance rebate is kept by the State to pay for your SERPS pension.

In 3 the State passes the rebate to your personal pension provider as a minimum contribution to your personal pension. As you don't want to pay extra optional contributions, your personal pension is what we'll call a 'minimum personal pension'.

On this basis you can look at the choice between 1 and 3 like this –

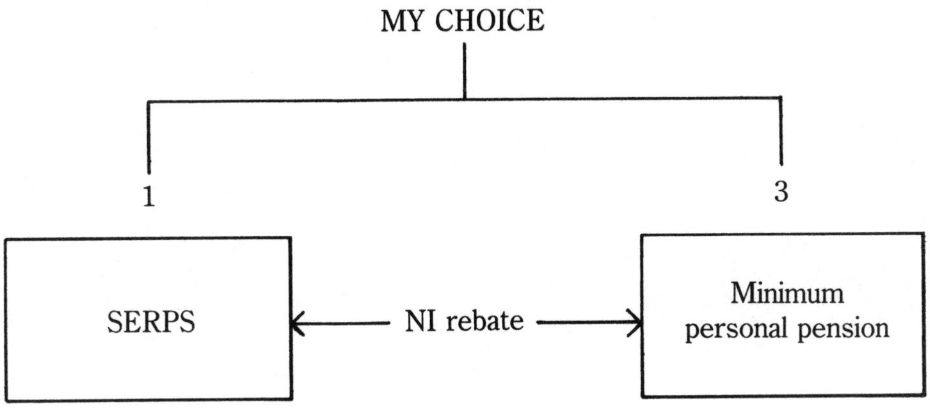

Question: Which is best? 1 or 3?
Answer: It depends how old you are.

As a personal pension is a money purchase scheme, the amount of pension you get from it depends on how much you pay in and how long it's invested for. The younger you are, the longer your contributions will be invested. So your personal fund will be bigger when you retire. The older you are, the shorter the period your contributions will be invested. So your personal fund will be smaller when you retire.

By making sensible assumptions about investment returns, the experts – known as 'actuaries' – can calculate a 'break-even' age, where a minimum personal pension can be expected to produce a personal pension equal to SERPS.

This 'break-even' age is generally thought to be about 48 if you're a man and about 42 if you're a woman. (If you get the 2% incentive mentioned on page 24 for five years, these ages increase to about 52 and about 47 respectively).

If you're over the 'break-even' age, it's probably better for you to contract in to SERPS.

If you're below the 'break-even' age, it's probably better for you to contract out of the SERPS and have a personal pension 'without' SERPS.

Remember, you can always contract back into SERPS when you reach the 'break-even' age.

That, then, is the position if you don't want to make contributions on top of the National Insurance rebate. But suppose you do want to contribute more (as we suggest you should if you can afford to)?

In that case you should consider the second choice.

SECOND CHOICE

This is the choice between 2 and 3.

The easiest way to look at this choice is like this –

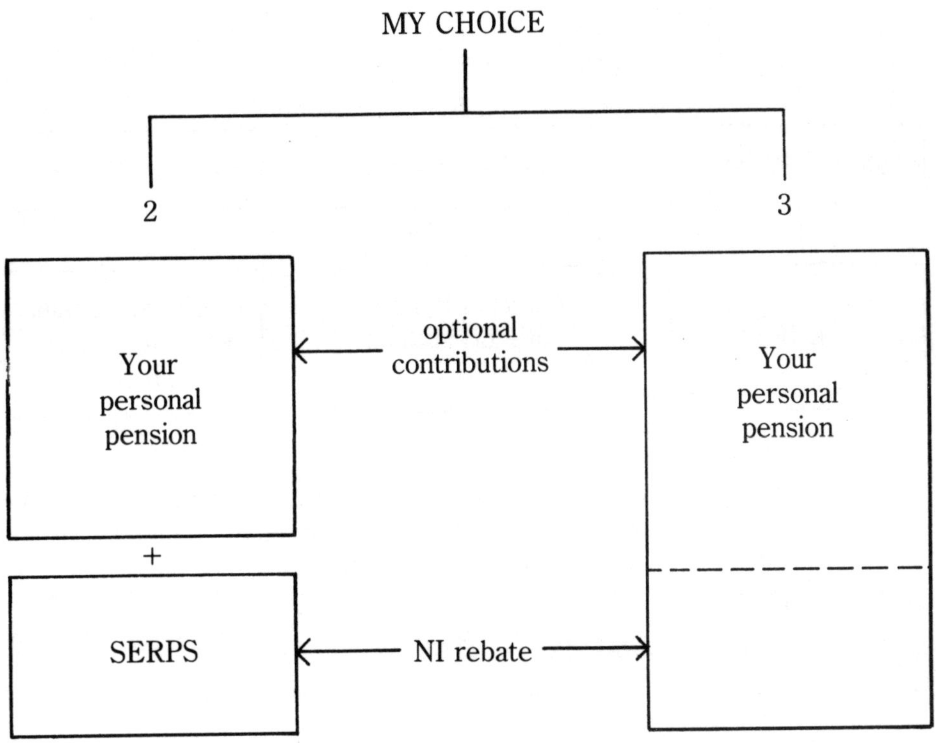

As you can see, this second choice is very different from the first. In 2 the optional extra contributions you pay go towards a personal pension which you have in addition to SERPS. In 3 they go to boost your minimum personal pension.

But **how** you make the choice is really just the same. That's because – assuming your optional contributions are of the same amount and the returns from the investments are similar – your age should still be the decisive factor.

In other words 2 is better if you're over the 'break-even' age we described when discussing the first choice, while 3 is better if you haven't yet reached it.

SITUATION 3 – I belong to or can join an employer scheme

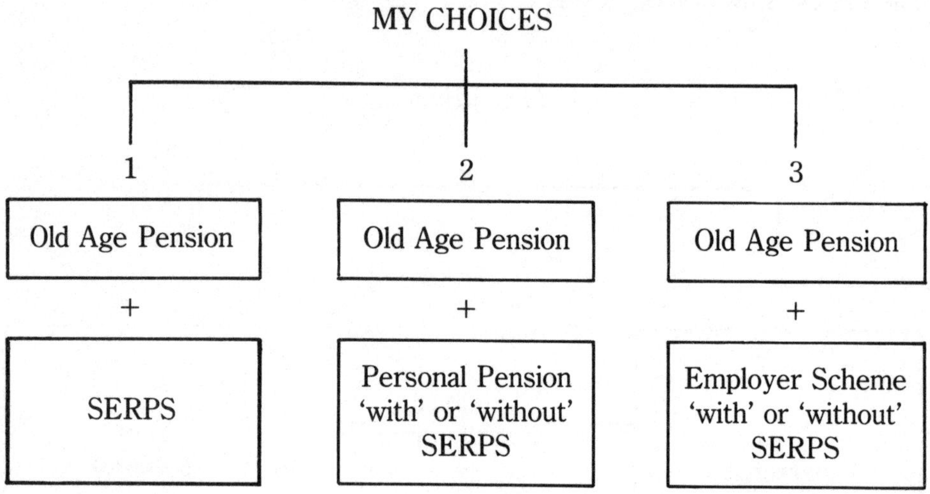

In this situation you're employed and – in contrast to Situation 2 – you **also** belong to or can join an employer scheme, which adds another important dimension. And employer schemes, like personal pensions, can be contracted into or out of SERPS.

So here you have the most choices of all.

FIRST CHOICE

Question: Should I choose 1 or 2?

Answer: If you compare this chart with the one on page 32, you will see that we have already dealt with this choice (though there we divided 2 into two halves).

But this chart also shows – see 3 – that we must now bring employer schemes into the picture.

SECOND CHOICE

Question: Should I choose 1 or 3?

Answer: If your employer's scheme is 'with' SERPS, choose 3. You will have a pension from your employer — to which he must contribute — as well as a SERPS pension.

3 has another advantage. On page 19 we pointed out the general rule that you can't belong to your employer's scheme and have a personal pension as well. We have drawn the chart opposite in a way which illustrates that general rule.

But this case is an exception — the **only** exception to that rule. Here you **can** have a personal pension as well as belonging to your employer's scheme, but only if you use your personal pension to contract out of SERPS and neither you nor your employer pays optional contributions on top of the National Insurance rebate.

In other words, it must be what on page 33 we called a minimum personal pension. Whether you should have a personal pension like this without SERPS or stay in SERPS through your employer's scheme depends on the principle of the 'break-even' age we described on page 34.

If your employer's scheme is 'without' SERPS we have to consider final salary and money purchase schemes separately.

Next question: Is a final salary employer scheme that's 'without' SERPS better than SERPS?

Answer: Normally yes. The benefits of final salary schemes must be at least as good as SERPS (see page 23) and in most cases are better.

Next question: Is a money purchase employer scheme that's 'without' SERPS better than SERPS?

Answer: We've already answered this! How so?

Remember two things –

* A personal 'pot' in a money purchase employer scheme works like the personal fund of a personal pension.

* Contributions to a money purchase employer scheme that's 'without' SERPS must be at least as big as the National Insurance rebate.

Now look at the chart on page 33. We can redraw it here like this

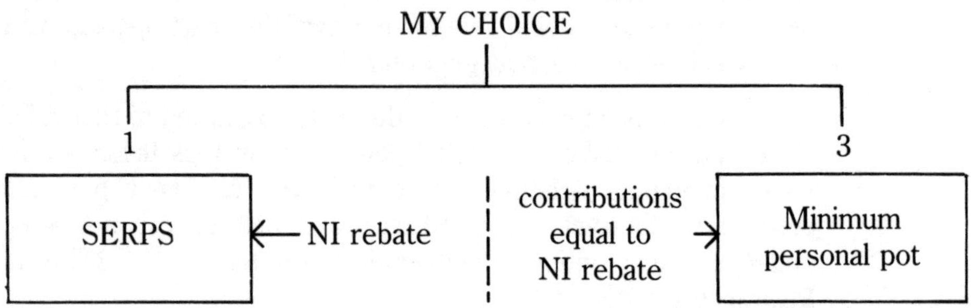

No doubt you can 'spot the difference'! But the principle of the 'break-even' age, which we described on page 34, applies here too.

However, the majority of money purchase employer schemes are designed to provide more than a minimum pension. For example, you and your employer may well pay more than minimum contributions, in which case 3 is always likely to be better than 1.

This leaves us to tackle the last, most important and most complex choice of all – the choice between 2 and 3.

THIRD CHOICE

Question: Should I choose 2 or 3?

THIS IS THE BIG DEBATE ABOUT EMPLOYER SCHEMES vs PERSONAL PENSIONS

It's important because the vast majority of people in pension schemes – some eleven million in total – belong to employer schemes and must now make this choice.

It's complex for the reasons that we'll look at now.

What Should I Ask About My Employer's Scheme?

Before you can decide whether or not a personal pension is a better bet for you than an employer scheme, you need to know the answers to some basic questions about your own employer's scheme.

You can fill in the answers to the questions below where indicated. It might be a good idea if you use a pencil – here and later in the book. You can then change any details if your employer makes major alterations to the scheme in a few years time or if you change jobs.

1 Is it:
(a) final salary
(b) money purchase
(c) hybrid?

2(i) If it is a final salary scheme, what fraction of my expected final earnings will I get for each year of service?

(ii) If it is a money purchase scheme
(a) what is my pension estimated to be in relation to my earnings at or close to retirement?
(b) what assumptions are being made about investment returns?
(c) what assumptions are being made about inflation between now and my normal retirement age?

(iii) If it is a hybrid scheme, how will my pension be calculated?

3 Is it 'with' or 'without' SERPS?

4 What percentage of my earnings do I pay as my contribution? %

5 What percentage of my earnings does my employer pay as his contribution? %

6 What is the normal retiring age?

7 When I retire and take my pension,
(a) what annual percentage increases to my pension are guaranteed? %
(b) what is my employer's record of making increases which are not guaranteed during the last 5 years?

8 If I die before I retire,
(a) what lump sum will my spouse get?
(b) what pension will my spouse get?
(c) will my children/other dependants get anything? YES/NO
(d) if yes, who and what?

9 If I die after I retire,
(a) what lump sum will my spouse get?
(b) what pension will my spouse get?
(c) will my children/other dependants get anything? YES/NO
(d) if yes, who and what?

10 What will happen if I have a long illness? Am I covered by permanent health insurance? YES/NO

---

11 What will I get if I have to retire early through ill health?

---

12 Are there any changes in the pipeline? YES/NO

If yes what changes?

---

13 If I don't join or leave my employer scheme and have a personal pension instead,

(a) will my employer contribute? YES/NO

(b) if yes, what percentage of my earnings? %

---

14 If I don't join or leave my employer scheme and have a personal pension instead,

(a) will my employer provide 'death benefits'? (see questions 8 and 9 above) YES/NO

(b) if yes, what benefits?

(c) will he provide 'ill health' benefits? (see questions 10 and 11 above) YES/NO

(d) if yes, what benefits?

15 If I don't join or leave my employer scheme and have a personal pension instead,

(a) will my employer let me join or rejoin his scheme? YES/NO

(b) if yes, on what conditions?

You'll probably find answers to some of these questions in the booklet about your employer's pension scheme which you should have been given soon after you joined it.

If you haven't got such a booklet, your employer should be able to give you one. Many employers are providing a lot of extra information about their pension schemes because they want their employees to know a lot more about them.

There may well be other questions that you'll want to add to cover circumstances that are particularly important in your own case. The ones we've listed here should help you start to find out the nuts and bolts of your employer's scheme.

If you're not sure of an answer, ask your employer, your pension fund manager, personnel officer or whoever is the appropriate person.

But remember that the law does not normally allow your employer or individual members of staff to advise you how to choose between your employer's scheme and a **particular** personal pension. This is because they are unlikely to be legally 'authorized' to do so. The law is not an ass – they cannot be expected to know about all the personal pensions on the market to give you expert, **specific** advice. So they couldn't protect your interests if they tried to do so.

They can only tell you about your employer scheme and advise you in **general** terms.

My Twenty Questions

To help you choose whether your employer's pension scheme or a personal pension is best suited to your individual needs we've highlighted twenty key questions that we suggest you work through one by one.

You'll see that after each question we've explained why we think it's important for you to consider it. Then we outline the main facts which we think are relevant to it. And finally we summarize what we think are the main points you should bear in mind in reaching your answer.

At the bottom of each question there are three boxes in which you can enter your answer. Tick the one that suits you best.

You might like to think of these twenty questions as a series of windows. Look through each window, one at a time – not at the house as a whole. That comes later.

I How young am I?

Your age is an important factor in deciding which type of pension scheme is better for you.

We saw earlier that age was important in choosing between a personal pension and SERPS, and we described what we called the 'break-even' age. A similar principle applies when comparing personal pensions (or money purchase employer schemes) with final salary employer schemes.

Final Salary Employer Schemes

The value of a final salary scheme increases with each year that you are in the scheme and every time that you have a pay rise – whether due to promotion or simply a cost of living increase. So every additional year of service near retirement age earns a bigger proportion of a bigger amount.

Money Purchase Employer Schemes and Personal Pensions

Your pension depends on the size of your personal 'pot' or personal fund when you retire. This depends on how much is paid in and for how long it is invested. For example, the value for your pension of £100 invested in your twenties is very much greater than the value of £100 invested in later life – say only five years before retirement.

The 'break-even' age between final salary schemes and money purchase arrangements is generally the early forties for men and the late thirties for women, but much depends on the level of contributions and the benefits provided by the employer scheme.

In terms of the amount of your pension, money purchase employer schemes and personal pensions are more suitable the younger you are. Final salary employer schemes are more suitable the older you are.

My answer to *this* question means that for me

My employer's scheme is better	
A personal pension is better	
It makes little difference for me either way	

Am I likely to change jobs frequently? 2

Changing jobs can affect your pension rights.

Final Salary Employer Schemes
As we saw on page 29, the cash value of your pension rights to date may not fully reflect your prospects if you'd stayed with your old employer. And it may not buy as many years service with your new employer as you have had with your old one – though you can boost your pension by paying AVCs.

If you leave your pension rights to date with your old employer, they may not be fully protected against inflation between the time you leave and the time you retire.

Money Purchase Employer Schemes and Personal Pensions
Changing jobs doesn't affect you. You can simply take your personal 'pot' or fund with you.

Final salary employer schemes are more suitable for those who don't change jobs frequently.

If you do change jobs frequently, money purchase employer schemes and personal pensions are a better bet – your pension rights are not affected.

My answer to *this* question means that for me

My employer's scheme is better	
A personal pension is better	
It makes little difference for me either way	

(See page 29)

3 How much will my employer contribute?

The more your employer contributes, the better for you.

Final Salary Employer Schemes
Your employer must contribute enough to meet the promise to pay you a pension of an amount which is defined as a proportion of your earnings at or close to your retirement – depending how long you've worked for him.

Money Purchase Employer Schemes
Your employer must contribute a defined amount.

Personal Pensions
Your employer doesn't have to contribute (apart from his share of the National Insurance rebate if your personal pension is 'without' SERPS).

What's more, many employers have indicated that they are unwilling to make contributions.

If you belong to an employer scheme, your employer must contribute towards your pension.

It seems likely that most employers won't contribute to personal pensions.

(See the answers to question 5 on page 40 and question 13 on page 41)

My answer to *this* question means that for me

My employer's scheme is better	
A personal pension is better	
It makes little difference for me either way	

How much can I contribute? 4

The more you pay in, the more you get out.

Employer Schemes

Your employer decides the amount of your normal contributions. (Some schemes are 'non-contributory' and the employer makes all the contributions).

The most you are allowed to contribute is 15% of your earnings – ignoring your employer's contributions.

Personal Pensions

You can decide how much you want to contribute.

You can pay up to a limit of 17½% of your earnings – more if you are over 50, up to a limit of 27½%. But here you can't ignore any contributions by your employer, because these limits apply to your combined contributions.

This may not matter much because most employers have said they won't contribute to a personal pension anyway!

You can normally contribute more to a personal pension than to an employer scheme.

My answer to *this* question means that for me

My employer's scheme is better	
A personal pension is better	
It makes little difference for me either way	

(See pages 27 and 28 and the answer to question 4 on page 39)

5 How much of my contributions goes towards my pension?

The more of your contributions that goes to build up your pension, the better.

Employer Schemes
Employer schemes are run on a group basis, so they enjoy the benefits of 'bulk buying' and of 'economies of scale' which simplify administration and reduce costs.

As a result more money is available to provide your pension benefits.

In many cases employers pay **all** the costs of administering their pension schemes.

Personal Pensions
Since personal pensions by their very nature are usually operated on an individual basis, the administration costs are normally likely to be higher. In addition there will be expenses to be covered from selling the pension. And in some cases commission is payable to a salesman.

So part of your pension is liable to be used to cover the costs of your personal pension provider and perhaps commission as well.

A greater share of your contributions is likely to go towards your pension if you belong to an employer scheme than if you have a personal pension.

(Questions 4 and 5 on page 72 cover important details on this point. You should refer to the answers to them when finalizing your decision on this).

My answer to *this* question means that for me

My employer's scheme is better	
A personal pension is better	
It makes little difference for me either way	

Can I pay extra money on top of my normal contributions?

6

If you pay extra money in, you get a bigger pension.

Employer Schemes
You can pay in-scheme AVCs to increase your pension from your employer scheme, but they must be combined with your normal contributions for the purpose of the limits we mentioned in answer to question 4.

Personal Pensions
With personal pensions there's no such thing as 'normal contributions'. To boost your pension you can simply pay in extra money to your personal fund, again subject to the limits mentioned in answer to question 4.

Whether you belong to an employer scheme or have a personal pension, you can increase your pension by paying in extra money – but there are different contribution limits.

My answer to *this* question means that for me

My employer's scheme is better	
A personal pension is better	
It makes little difference for me either way	

(See page 21)

7 Can I pay extra money to a personal pension plan of my own as well as belonging to my employer's scheme?

There are advantages in having the best of both worlds.

We've already mentioned that you can boost your pension from your employer's scheme by paying into a free-standing AVC scheme of your own.

This can give you a wider choice of savings possibilities. You might wish to use your AVC contributions for a type of investment not available in your employer scheme – for example a unit linked investment which gives you scope for higher returns (though with higher risk) through investing in the Stock Exchange. Alternatively you might choose to start an AVC scheme with a building society to have the convenience of calling in to make small or irregular payments whenever it suits you.

Free-standing AVCs enable you to retain the benefits of an employer scheme and at the same time boost your pension with flexible arrangements to meet your own particular needs.

Remember, you can only have a personal pension if you don't belong to an employer scheme (unless your employer's scheme is 'with' SERPS, in which case you *can* have a 'minimum personal pension' as well).

(See pages 21 and 37 and the answer to Question 3 on page 39)

My answer to *this* question means that for me

My employer's scheme is better	
A personal pension is better	
It makes little difference for me either way	

Can I have a pension mortgage? 8

If you have a pension mortgage, you'll have a smaller pension.

With a pension mortgage you use your pension scheme to help you pay your mortgage.

You don't repay your mortgage until you retire, but you pay interest on the whole of the sum you borrow. This enables you to get tax relief on the interest at the highest rate of income tax you pay (subject to the £30,000 limit which applies to mortgages generally).

You also enjoy the normal tax advantages of a pension scheme. Your own contributions obtain relief at the highest rate of income tax you pay and the lump sum which you take when you retire is tax free.

When you retire, you convert enough of your pension into a lump sum to enable you to pay off your loan. Of course, you can pay off some of the loan in another way – for example by moving to a less expensive house and using the difference in the price to pay some of it off.

Although you mustn't legally bind yourself to use your pension in this way, it's generally possible to have one whether you belong to an employer scheme or have a personal pension – subject to the limits for the lump sums set out on pages 27 and 28.

It's possible to have a pension mortgage whether you belong to an employer scheme or have a personal pension.

But it's very important to remember that you cannot use your pension to provide a big house *and* a big pension. If you use a substantial part of your pension to pay for your house, your pension will be considerably reduced.

My answer to *this* question means that for me

My employer's scheme is better	
A personal pension is better	
It makes little difference for me either way	

9 What happens if I am ill before I retire?

A good pension to live on can be vital if you are forced to retire early because you are too ill to work.

If you are ill and unable to work, you will receive statutory sick pay from the State. However, many employers operate schemes to make up your earnings to the normal level and continue to pay contributions towards your pension as if you were still working. Your employer may also increase your earnings to take some account of inflation.

If your employer doesn't operate a scheme like this, you may be forced to take early retirement. This can have serious consequences, particularly if you are relatively young when forced to retire and haven't built up significant pension entitlements.

Final Salary Employer Schemes

If illness forces you to retire early, your pension would usually be reduced because it would be starting from a younger age than normal and you wouldn't have completed the normal length of service.

Final salary schemes often offer generous terms in this situation. Frequently no reduction is made because of the earlier starting date. In many cases the employee will also be credited with some or all of the extra years of service which he or she would otherwise have been able to complete.

Money Purchase Employer Schemes

If you are forced to retire early, all you will have in this case is the amount built up in your own personal 'pot'. If you are fairly near retirement age this might be quite adequate, but if you are much younger, it may buy only a small pension.

Employers who operate money purchase schemes may also be generous in improving the position for those forced to retire early by paying an additional sum.

Personal Pensions

If you have a personal pension, you're again restricted to the amount built up in your personal fund. In this case, however, your employer is less likely to pay extra to help you increase your pension.

You can obtain some alternative protection by taking out 'permanent health insurance'. But you'll have to pay the premiums yourself, which will reduce the amount you can afford to pay towards your personal pension. You may also have to pass a medical examination.

Employer schemes often provide valuable protection against illness and early retirement due to illness.

With a personal pension you are more likely to have to take out insurance at extra cost to yourself.

My answer to *this* question means that for me

My employer's scheme is better	
A personal pension is better	
It makes little difference for me either way	

(See the answers to questions 10 and 14 (c) and (d) on page 41)

10 What happens if I die before I retire?

You would be very irresponsible if you did not make quite sure that your family would have enough to live on if you die before you retire.

It's always tempting to think that there's little chance of your dying before you retire. But, sadly, many people **do** die in harness and even if you're in the best of health an unlucky accident could carry you off tomorrow.

If you're single and there's no one depending on you, you don't have to worry about death benefits. If you're the bread-winner, though, or one of them, married and perhaps with young children, what are your dependants going to live on if you die?

Employer Schemes

Your employer scheme is almost certain to provide death benefits if you die before you retire. These usually take the form of a lump sum which might be two, three or even four times your annual earnings and which will go to your spouse along with a regular pension. Sometimes there will also be a pension for your children.

Thanks to the number of employees covered, employer schemes have the advantage of bulk insurance cover which reduces the cost and often includes all employees no matter what their state of health. The important point is that these costs are your employer's – there's no extra cost to you.

Personal Pensions

If you choose to leave, or not to join, your employer's scheme and do your own thing by having a personal pension, your employer may well not cover you at all for death benefits.

If you aren't covered by your employer and you die before you retire, all your spouse will get is what's in your personal fund at the time of your death, which may not be very much, especially if you are young. So you should arrange life cover yourself – at extra cost to you and without the economies of scale which an employer scheme benefits from.

This may mean that you won't be able to afford to pay as much to your own personal pension as you might wish.

If you're in poor health, you may find it difficult to get cover at all.

Death benefits that cost you nothing are a major advantage of employer schemes.

If you have a personal pension and your employer doesn't cover you for death benefits, you have to pay extra to buy your own life assurance, which means you have less to contribute towards your personal pension.

(See the answer to question 8 on page 40 and question 14 (a) and (b) on page 41)

My answer to *this* question means that for me

My employer's scheme is better	
A personal pension is better	
It makes little difference for me either way	

11 What happens when I die after I retire?

Here too you would be very irresponsible if you didn't make quite sure that your spouse – and other dependants – have enough to live on when you die after you retire.

Employer Schemes
Your employer scheme will almost certainly provide a spouse's pension, usually amounting to half of what you were being paid when you died. In addition an employer scheme often provides pensions for children and other dependants.

Personal Pensions
As well as using your personal fund to buy a pension for yourself, you can, if you want to, buy a pension for your spouse and other dependants to start when you die. (If your personal pension is 'without' SERPS, half of the part derived from the National Insurance rebate **must** carry on being paid to your spouse after your death.)

Of course, if you use some of your personal fund to buy death benefits like this it means that there will be less to spend on a pension for yourself.

Most employer schemes automatically provide a pension for your spouse and other dependants at no extra cost to you.

If you have a personal pension, you can decide to distribute your personal fund between a pension for yourself and a pension for your spouse and other dependants. But if you do so, your own pension will be smaller.

(See the answer to question 9 on page 40)

My answer to *this* question means that for me

My employer's scheme is better	
A personal pension is better	
It makes little difference for me either way	

Will my pension increase during my retirement? 12

If your pension doesn't increase during your retirement and there is a rise in prices, your standard of living could decline as you get older.

Employer Schemes

Many employer schemes guarantee to increase pensions once they start to be paid by, say, 3% or 4% per year. (If your employer scheme is 'without' SERPS, the part of your pension which you've earned since 6 April 1988 must increase by at least 3% a year (or the rise in prices if less).) If the guaranteed rate falls behind the rise in prices, many employers give extra increases if they can afford it.

There are some schemes that guarantee to increase pensions in line with the rise in prices.

Many schemes, which don't guarantee to increase pensions at all, do in fact increase them – at no extra cost to the employees.

Personal Pensions

You can arrange for your personal pension to increase by whatever percentage you like. (If your personal pension is 'without' SERPS, the part derived from the National Insurance rebate must increase by at least 3% a year (or the rise in prices if less).)

With a personal pension, though, you can only use the amount of money in your personal fund. The cost of buying increases means that you will start off with a smaller pension.

Many employer schemes increase pensions to a reasonable extent in relation to the rise in prices.

With a personal pension you have to buy increases yourself which means starting off with a smaller pension. The greater the future increases, the smaller the pension you start with.

My answer to *this* question means that for me

My employer's scheme is better	
A personal pension is better	
It makes little difference for me either way	

13 What happens if I retire earlier than normal?

If you want or have to retire earlier than normal retirement age, you'll need enough to live on.

Question 9 dealt with early retirement as a result of illness. However you may find that you want to stop working and start receiving your pension early, so that you can pursue another career, or retire and do all the other things that you've always wanted but been too busy to do. On the other hand you may be unlucky and be forced to retire, whether you want to or not, because you've been made redundant.

Employer Schemes

If you want to retire earlier than normal, you can do so from the age of 50, though normally your employer must agree to this. (If your employer scheme is 'without' SERPS, the part of your pension which replaces SERPS can't be paid until you are 65 if you're a man, or 60 if you're a woman.)

If you leave early, your pension is usually reduced – firstly because the contributions have been paid for a shorter time and secondly because the smaller amount of money will have to pay for a pension covering a longer period of retirement.

Some employer schemes offer more generous early retirement pensions in certain circumstances – for example if you are retiring within five years of your normal retirement age, or if your employer has asked you to retire early or made you redundant.

Personal Pensions

You can take your personal pension at any time from the age of 50. (If your personal pension is 'without' SERPS, the part derived from the National Insurance rebate is subject to the same restrictions as those for employer schemes 'without' SERPS and can't be paid to men until they are 65, or to women until they reach 60.)

However, the earlier you want to take your pension, the earlier you will stop making contributions. So you'll get a smaller pension because you'll have less money in your pension fund to buy an annuity with more instalments.

Employer schemes are generally more flexible than personal pensions with regard to early retirement.

(See the answer to question 6 on page 40)

My answer to *this* question means that for me

My employer's scheme is better	
A personal pension is better	
It makes little difference for me either way	

14 What happens if I retire later than normal?

You may want to stay on at work after your normal retirement age because you like working or can't afford to retire.

Employer Schemes

You can stay on at work after your normal retirement age if your employer agrees.

If you do, you will get a bigger pension because it will be starting later and will be paid for a shorter time.

Personal Pensions

You can carry on making contributions to the age of 75 so long as you continue working, which of course is subject to your employer's agreement.

If you do retire later, the situation with a personal pension is much the same as with employer schemes – you will get a bigger pension because you will have more money in your personal fund to buy an annuity with fewer instalments.

Here there's probably little to choose between an employer scheme and a personal pension.

My answer to *this* question means that for me

My employer's scheme is better	
A personal pension is better	
It makes little difference for me either way	

(See the answer to question 6 on page 40)

What happens if there is severe inflation before I retire? 15

Severe inflation before you retire can ruin your old age if the pension you start with when you retire hasn't kept up with the rise in prices.

Final Salary Employer Schemes

You're not likely to have a great problem on this score. Your pension will be related to your annual earnings at or close to your retirement and earnings tend to keep up with the rise in prices.

Your employer is unlikely to have allowed for unexpectedly high inflation, so he will probably have to increase his contributions to meet the cost of keeping your pension in line with your final earnings.

Money Purchase Employer Schemes and Personal Pensions

Here it depends on how much has been put in, the way in which your personal 'pot' or personal fund has been invested and whether the return on the investments has kept up with inflation.

A final salary employer scheme is a safer bet to cope with severe inflation before you retire than a money purchase employer scheme or a personal pension.

My answer to *this* question means that for me

My employer's scheme is better	
A personal pension is better	
It makes little difference for me either way	

16 What happens if there is severe inflation after I retire?

Severe inflation after you retire can also ruin your old age if your pension doesn't keep up with the rise in prices.

(Turn back to question 12 and you'll find that this has been partly answered already).

Employer Schemes
Some schemes guarantee to increase your pension in line with inflation after you retire. In other cases, many good employers would try to protect you against severe inflation.

Personal Pensions
You can arrange for the pension you start with to increase year by year, provided that you start from a lower base. The more you want your pension to increase, the lower your starting pension will have to be. It is possible to buy a personal pension that will increase in line with inflation but that is relatively expensive.

Employer schemes are likely to provide a better safeguard against severe inflation after you retire than personal pensions.

My answer to *this* question means that for me

My employer's scheme is better	
A personal pension is better	
It makes little difference for me either way	

What happens if annuity rates are low when I retire?

17

If annuity rates are low when you retire, your standard of living in your old age could also be low.

Annuity rates rise and fall broadly in line with changes in interest rates in the financial market. These interest rates can vary quite suddenly, producing large and unexpected changes in annuity rates.

Final Salary Employer Schemes
As a final salary scheme promises a pension defined in relation to your annual earnings at or close to retirement, you needn't worry if annuity rates are low when you retire. Your pension is usually paid from the income from the fund, and not by buying an annuity. In any case, it's your employer who has to do the worrying, as he must carry the cost of any shortfall in order to meet the promise made to you.

Money Purchase Employer Schemes and Personal Pensions
Your personal 'pot' or fund must be used to buy an annuity, so if annuity rates are low when you retire you will simply get a smaller pension.

Your pension from a final salary employer scheme is not affected if annuity rates are low when you retire.

Money purchase employer schemes and personal pensions provide little safeguard if annuity rates are low. But they could do better if (who knows?) annuity rates are high.

My answer to *this* question means that for me

My employer's scheme is better	
A personal pension is better	
It makes little difference for me either way	

18 What happens if the value of the investments on which my pension depends falls before I retire?

A fall in the value of the investments on which your pension depends could mean a fall in your standard of living in your old age.

Final Salary Employer Schemes

A fall in the value of the investments in your employer's pension fund shouldn't affect you. True, there will be less money in the fund to provide your pension, but it won't necessarily affect the income from the fund needed to provide the pension. Any extra cost will fall on your employer, because he has promised you a pension which is defined in relation to your salary at or close to your retirement.

Money Purchase Employer Schemes and Personal Pensions

If the value of the investments in your personal 'pot' or fund falls, there will be less money available to buy your pension. So it all depends how stable the investments are.

If, for example, you have a personal pension which is the deposit type and so depends on earning interest, a fall in the value of investments should make little difference.

If your personal pension is a with-profits type, you might well start getting smaller bonuses and so end up with a smaller personal fund which would buy a smaller annuity.

The unit-linked type of personal pension would suffer the most. Your personal fund would be smaller and would buy a smaller annuity.

What is obviously desirable is that your money should be invested in stable investments as you near your retirement.

Final salary employer schemes provide a secure safeguard against a fall in the value of investments in your employer's pension fund.

Money purchase employer schemes and personal pensions are generally less secure though it depends on the way the personal 'pot' or fund is invested.

My answer to *this* question means that for me

My employer's scheme is better	
A personal pension is better	
It makes little difference for me either way	

19 If I choose a personal pension, will my employer let me join (or rejoin) his scheme if I later change my mind?

It may be better for you to belong to an employer scheme later on in your working life, even if you prefer a personal pension now.

The balance of advantage and disadvantage between different types of pension scheme can change with your age and other circumstances.

Growing older is inevitable, but other changes are less predictable. For instance, will you get married? Will you have children? Will you become better off? Will you become more settled in your job?

That's why it's important before choosing a personal pension to find out if your employer will let you join or rejoin his scheme at a later date.

If he is prepared to let you do this, you should find out what conditions may apply. For instance, you might have to apply or reapply before a certain age, say 35 or 40. You might have to provide evidence of satisfactory health – and perhaps pay for the medical examination yourself – to qualify for ill health and death benefits. Different employers will take different views on these questions.

Before you choose a personal pension, it is essential to look ahead to the consequences, to make sure that you are not closing any options which may be important to you in the future -- like the option to join or rejoin your employer's scheme.

(See the answer to question 15 on page 42)

My answer to *this* question means that for me

My employer's scheme is better	
A personal pension is better	
It makes little difference for me either way	

What sort of person am I? 20

It's important to remember that profiting from your pension planning isn't *just* a question of trying to calculate how big your pension will be. You're a human being after all.

However, you're not alone in facing the question of whether to belong to your employer's pension scheme or have a personal pension instead. Eleven million other people, men and women in all walks of life and all sorts of jobs, are having to answer the same question for themselves.

Some can afford to pay more towards their pension than others. Some have no dependants to be cared for; others have the responsibilities of family life. Some are young; some not so young! Some people enjoy changing jobs, while others prefer to be settled in the same one for all or most of their working lives. There are those who can't bear the thought of stopping work and those who can scarcely contain themselves until retirement day.

All the previous questions have looked at the way in which differences like these may affect the difficult choice you have to make. Here you face the most personal and probably the most challenging question of all. Are you prepared to take risks, or would you prefer to know where you stand? Do you prefer doing your own thing, or do you feel a need to identify with colleagues at work and have your employer standing behind you? Do you really want to go to all the trouble of making your own arrangements, or are you content to rely on your employer to arrange things for you?

We're not suggesting that you should base your decision on considerations like these if the right choice is clear on other grounds.

However, we think it's fair to say that other things being equal, or if you're in doubt about which path to follow, you probably won't go far wrong if you do what makes you feel comfortable inside. In this sense peace of mind must be important. You're only human.

No one can advise you with this one. Only you know the answer, but it's a question you might spend a moment or two reflecting on after all the others.

My answer to *this* question means that for me

My employer's scheme is better	
A personal pension is better	
It makes little difference for me either way	

Summary of My Twenty Questions

Now that you've worked your way through your 'Twenty Questions' one by one, look at the summary opposite and transfer the ticks you have made in the boxes for each question to one or other of the columns under the heading 'Present Situation' according to which of the first two boxes you have ticked. If you have ticked the third box, then leave both columns blank or put a line through them.

We don't suggest that you should reach a decision simply by adding up the ticks and seeing which column wins – some questions will be much more important to you than others. However, the summary will help you to see at a glance **which** ones you do consider to be important and to weigh up the pros and cons.

Summary of My Twenty Questions

	PRESENT SITUATION		CHANGED SITUATION	
	Employer Scheme	Personal Pension	Employer Scheme	Personal Pension
1 Age				
2 Job-changing				
3 Employer's contributions				
4 My normal contributions				
5 Do they all go to my pension?				
6 Extra contributions				
7 Free-standing AVCs				
8 Pension mortgages				
9 Ill-health				
10 Death before retirement				
11 Death after retirement				
12 Pension increases				
13 Early retirement				
14 Late retirement				
15 Inflation before retirement				
16 Inflation after retirement				
17 Annuity rates				
18 Fall in value of investments				
19 Rejoining my employer's scheme				
20 Personal attitude				

Is My Employer Planning to Change His Scheme?

Changes to your employer's scheme might be enough to make you change your mind about whether your employer's scheme or a personal pension is better for you.

Look back to question 12 on page 41 and you'll see whether any changes are in the pipeline.

If so, look back to the **Twenty Questions.** Which of the boxes have you ticked at the end of each one? If your employer makes some or all of the changes he is planning, will you change your answers to any of them? If you decide you will, fill in the answers again but this time in the columns under 'Changed Situation'.

If, when you've done this, you see that the planned changes could alter your decision, discuss the position with your employer.

What Should I Ask a Personal Pension Salesman?

If your conclusion at this stage is to consider buying a personal pension, there are still quite a few questions you should ask a personal pension salesman before finally making up your mind what to do. (It may also be wise to talk to more than one salesman.)

On page 42 we pointed out that your employer and his staff could probably only advise you in **general** terms, because they are not likely to be expert enough to give you **specific** advice about your choice between a **particular** personal pension and your employer's scheme. So they are not likely to be authorized to do so.

The legal position is quite different for personal pension salesmen.

Since personal pension salesmen are not just giving **general** advice but each is seeking to persuade you to buy a **particular** scheme, they have to comply with strict laws to protect your interests. Amongst other things, they must know all about your personal circumstances and your employer's scheme. Knowing all that, they must give you the best advice.

In addition they can **either** sell their **own** companies' personal pensions, **or** be entirely independent and sell you the best (from your point of view) of all the personal pensions on the market. In either case they must advise you that the personal pensions they are recommending are better for you than your employer's scheme.

This means that a personal pension salesman (or his or her employer) must be 'authorized' to sell personal pensions by one or other of the organizations set up to ensure that these laws are complied with and that your interests are protected.

If a salesman is not 'authorized' he or she is committing a serious offence under the law.

Bearing all this in mind, we suggest that you put the following questions to any personal pensions salesman you are dealing with.

Questions To My Personal Pensions Salesman

1 Are you (or your employer) authorized to sell personal pensions?

____

2 Are you selling the products of one personal pension provider or advising me that this is the best personal pension for me out of all those available?

____

____

____

3 (a) Are you advising that this personal pension is better for me than my employer's scheme?

____

(b) If you are, what are the main reasons for this advice?

____

____

____

____

4 What commission will you and your employer get if I buy this personal pension?

Salesman ______________________________

Employer ______________________________

5 What other charges (administration charges, etc) will be deducted from my contributions?

Administrative charges ______________________________

Other charges ______________________________

6 What do you estimate my pension will be in relation to my earnings at or close to my retirement?

____

7 What assumptions are you making about investment returns?

____

8 What assumptions are you making about inflation between now and my normal retirement age?

____

9 (a) What is the investment record of the company whose personal pension you are selling over the last 10 years?

(b) How does that record compare with inflation over the last 10 years?

10 What 'death benefits' will there be if I die before I retire?

11 What 'death benefits' will there be if I die after I retire?

12 What happens if I have a long illness?
Am I covered by permanent health insurance?

13 What happens if I have to retire early through ill-health?

14 What happens if I stop paying towards this personal pension after

1 year

2 years

5 years

10 years

Should I Discuss My Choice With Anyone?

We think you should. After all you're making a very important decision that may have far-reaching consequences.

It's also perfectly understandable that you may still have doubts and conflicts in your mind about the choice you ought to make. The issues are complex and sorting out your priorities and needs now and in the years to come is a complicated process – especially if you're getting different advice from your employer and a personal pension salesman.

Your employer may have said in **general** terms that his was a good scheme for you and that he thinks you would be unwise to leave it. On the other hand one or more personal pension salesmen may have said that a **particular** personal pension would be better for you than your employer's scheme.

In any event, we think there are two further steps you should take before settling on your choice.

The first is another question worth considering. Maybe now's the time to ask your spouse and other dependants what they think about your pension planning (if you haven't consulted them already)? Get them to read this book, look at your answers, and talk through them with you, so that you can agree together what route you should go down.

The second we put very positively. Although the final decision rests with you and your dependants alone, you'd be wise to seek truly independent professional advice tailored to suit all your particular circumstances. The trouble is that independent advice may be scarce – and expensive!

The main principle behind getting genuinely independent advice is to speak to an adviser who charges a fee for his or her advice and not to one who may be influenced by the potential receipt of commission.

As the whole question of pensions is becoming such an important topic, some firms of accountants, solicitors and independent brokers may have a specialist in pension matters. Many of the members of the following two organisations are also willing to work for you on the independent fee-paying basis which we have suggested is so important:

Society of Pensions Consultants,
Ludgate House,
Ludgate Circus,
London EC4A 2AB

The Association of Consulting Actuaries,
Watson House,
London Road,
Reigate,
Surrey RH2 9PQ

The Next Step

By now you'll have all the facts and figures you need. You'll have seen what the main types of pension scheme can provide and what their limitations are. You'll also see that in principle there are literally dozens of combinations you could choose from. In working your way through to this point you'll have ruled out many of them already and to help boil down the remaining options here are the last three questions to ask yourself...

What is available to me?

One of the many details you'll have discovered by this stage is exactly what options are open to you and these are obviously the only ones you'll be able to choose from. For example, if your employer doesn't operate a pension scheme, then the only tricky decision you have to make is between a personal pension and SERPS.

Which is going to best suit my needs?

It's horses for courses! And it's quite probable that different types of pension scheme will be more suitable at different stages of your life. As you near retirement the security of a more stable type of pension like a final salary employer scheme, or a personal pension of the deposit type may be more appealing than the rather more risky arrangements that may have attracted you when you were younger. Don't forget either the benefits of a hybrid scheme (see page 18), which could offer you the best of both worlds.

Which is the best value for money?

The crucial factor behind any pension planning is that it should be just that – planning for your pension. In essence a pension scheme is a long-term arrangement that's going to provide benefits in the future, with additional cover and security from now until retirement as a bonus. By the time you reach retirement it's going to be too late to begin making provision for it. So 'value for money' isn't simply a matter of which scheme costs less at the moment. With SERPS or a minimum personal pension, you can keep the amount you contribute to a pension to a minimum. The snag is that you'll also receive pretty nearly the minimum when you come to rely on it in your old age. You get out what you put in – and don't forget that in an employer scheme you'll also benefit from the contributions your employer makes on your behalf.

It's also important not to lose sight of the fact that when you do come to retire there's a very good chance that your full pension will be made up of bits and pieces from several sources. Don't forget to keep track of **all** of these providers, not just for your own benefit, but for your dependants in case they have to contact them should anything happen to you. Let each pension source know your change of address every time you move house and see that at least one member of your family knows where you keep your pension papers.

Armed with this book and your own answers to the questions it poses, you'll be in a strong position to talk to a salesman and an independent adviser. You'll have the right questions to ask them literally at your fingertips and you can be confident that you'll understand their answers!

The Way Ahead

Not only has working with this book shown me clearly and concisely how the various types of pension scheme work and what they have to offer, it's convinced me that really getting involved in planning my own pension strategy is immensely stimulating and rewarding.

It's thought provoking too. **Future Perfect** has made me consider questions about myself and my future that have given a fresh new perspective to my years ahead. For the first time I can see a logical and practical means of making hopes, ambitions and pipe-dreams for later life concrete realities.

I know what achieving these is going to cost. I know what my wife and children are going to receive if fate robs me of the chance to enjoy the fruits of my plans in person. And I know how to keep a check on my changing circumstances and act accordingly.

Now I've got the answers, I'm convinced that I'm going to get the very best from my pension – in every way – and that reading this book has shown you the way ahead to make your future perfect too.

Here's to retirement!